SWEET WORLD

SWEET WORLD

Maureen Seaton

CavanKerry
PRESS

CavanKerry Press Ltd.
Fort Lee, New Jersey
www.cavankerrypress.org

Publisher's Cataloging-In-Publication Data
(Prepared by The Donohue Group, Inc.)
Names: Seaton, Maureen, 1947- author.
Title: Sweet world / Maureen Seaton.
Other Titles: Laurel books.
Description: First edition. | Fort Lee, New Jersey : CavanKerry Press, 2019.
Identifiers: ISBN 9781933880723
Subjects: LCSH: Seaton, Maureen, 1947- —Health—Poetry. | Breast—Cancer—
    Psychological aspects—Poetry. | Women—Psychology—Poetry.
Classification: LCC PS3569.E218 S94 2019 | DDC 811/.54—dc23

Book design and typesetting by Mayfly Design
First Edition 2019, Printed in the United States of America

Sweet World is the 13th title of CavanKerry's Literature of Illness imprint. LaurelBooks are fine collections of poetry and prose that explore the many poignant issues associated with confronting serious physical and/or psychological illness.

CavanKerry Press is grateful for the support it receives from the New Jersey State Council on the Arts.

ALSO BY MAUREEN SEATON

Fisher (2018)
Tit, with Blue Guitar (chapbook) (2016)
Fibonacci Batman: New & Selected Poems 1991–2011 (2013)
Genetics (2012)
Cave of the Yellow Volkswagen (2009)
America Loves Carney (chapbook) (2009)
Sex Talks to Girls: A Memoir (2008)
Venus Examines Her Breast (2004)
Little Ice Age (2001)
Miss Molly Rockin' (chapbook) (1998)
Furious Cooking (1996)
The Sea among the Cupboards (1992)
Fear of Subways (1991)

CO-AUTHORED

Caprice: Collected, Uncollected, and New Collaborations (with Denise Duhamel)
    (2015)
Two Thieves & a Liar (with Neil de la Flor & Kristine Snodgrass) (2012)
Sinéad O'Connor and Her Coat of a Thousand Bluebirds (with Neil de la Flor)
    (2011)
Stealth (with Samuel Ace) (2011)
Facial Geometry (chapbook, with Neil de la Flor & Kristine Snodgrass)
    (2006)
Little Novels (chapbook, with Denise Duhamel) (2002)
Oyl (chapbook, with Denise Duhamel) (2000)
Exquisite Politics (with Denise Duhamel) (1997)

CO-EDITED

Reading Queer: Poetry in a Time of Chaos (with Neil de la Flor) (2018)
Saints of Hysteria: A Half-Century of Collaborative American Poetry (with
    Denise Duhamel & David Trinidad) (2007)

for Sebastian

Contents

Ghosts run right through me and keep running—down to the river for a drink, up a hollow tree. Touched like this, I am nevertheless clothed and breathing, opaque and pounding with blood—and when the ghosts hang their slips in the black oaks I call out. Leaves float down and cover my feet. Ghosts sit in the trees videotaping. Spiders spin lace around my breasts.

Fore/words: 2017

There Was Once a Woman in This Room

For much of 2014 and 2015 I lived down the street from a magical lake in a magical house near magical mountains with a family of Coloradans I can only (yup) call magical. It was in this house—in fact, in a magical room up the stairs with a sloped ceiling and snow-themed sheets—that I got through the surreal ordeal and terrifying decision-making of breast cancer treatment, having driven alone from South Florida with two lumps in my left breast (two different cancers, I was told), and having signed on with a crew of young women docs in the magical, if laughably magical, bubble of Boulder—where I'd never been in my life, and where I'd traveled in a hazy blackout of the cancer-induced variety, to get well.

During this time I wrote constantly. I wrote like I would never be able to think, much less write, again. I wrote science and ultraviolet, I wrote spirit and place. I wrote everything in poems, of course—I couldn't think beyond metaphor. Some days I wrote with my tongue planted in my cheek, making light of snow, of skiers, of myself, of fear. I didn't intend to make light of cancer—mine or anyone else's—but I did intend to make light. Lots of it. Given that mortality was sudden and focused and within walking distance, I tried constantly to make light for however long the journey.

Now I'm back in Miami, walking on (salt) water again, this time with one breast, recalling that sunny snowy magical place and its people who loved me fiercely those many months and beyond. I hope you will forgive me, dear reader, if I've mixed up magic with grief, love with terror, light with impenetrable dark.

Tit, with Shelf Life

I think of it as a tiny Earth. A typhoon in a glass globe.

I think of it as blood beneath a door, faces on a vaulted ceiling.

I think of it as a severed head, toe bone of a sloth.

I think of it as frightened, a twitchy metaphor, frightening. (Boo!)

I think of it as a random bird impaled on a random tree. (Hawthorn.)

I think of it as a celestial non-sphere: Phobos (fear) or Deimos (terror).

I think of it as a soul unraveling, newly dead (or newly born).

I think of it as a rogue wave, a (God) particle accelerator.

I think of it as a pit harboring a fruit tree. (Plum.)

I think of it as Ω or π or any transcendental body. (Uncountable.)

I think of it as Pu sliding off a freight train. (Plutonium.)

I think of it as a haunting, a bell tower. (A bell.)

I think of it as a pike with ulcerous flesh and missing eye.

I think of it as a cell whispering: *I am in everything. Everything am I.*

I Dreamt a Land of Someone Else's Invention

It was a time for big decisions, so I followed four
ghostly Mustangs doing 95 on I-70 into Colorado.

I saw snow geese heading in opposite directions,
passing through each other's flight patterns

like subatomic particles or the sudden astral bodies
of Americans killed last year by other Americans

with assault weapons, and I knew it was a sign,
geese and Mustangs shadowing each other in and

out of formation like sylphs. I loved them. Who
wouldn't? Just east of Denver the blizzard hit

and we all slowed to crawling, even the semis,
even the Range Rovers. We fishtailed and jackknifed

through Limon until half of us were upside down
on the median, the other half praying and peeing.

My dream, or whoever's dream, had not prepared me
for death, though I'd witnessed the palindrome geese

and the phantom Mustangs. My wheels were in motion
in a way that reminded me of a marriage I'd failed at

for twenty-five years. So I pulled off in Byers
and got a room at the Budget Host Longhorn Motel

from a man who looked like a snow angel who said:
We only have two kings left. I lay down on one and slept.

Two Men Walking a Breast

Or things that might give you cancer

(1)

Fluorescent light, UV light, computer light, Crystal Light.
Nightlight in the shape of a pig light or a llama light.

Saccharin, of course. (Poor mice).   DDT, MSG, and HFCS.
You could get it if you're old.   Or a woman.   Or young.

If your period came late the first time or if you went through
menopause late   or early.   Those wires outside the nursery

window, the ones attached to the pole in your backyard?
That's right.   Also: chemotherapy.   (How rude.)

Estrogen could give it to you.   Hormones and hi-lines
in general.   Pots, pans, deodorants, charcoal, quantum

(2)

jumps, spider bites, time travel.   It could also be contagious.
(Don't stand too close to your flat screen, for that matter.)

Your microwave could zap it to you.   Living in a desert
could bequeath it to you if a big bomb was dropped there.

Nuclear waste on a highway: Duh.   Nuclear waste in
general: Duh^2.   Therefore: radiation treatment.   (What?)

Certain (many) rivers. (Keep hands inside kayak.)   Being
too nice could definitely give it to you.   Trips to IKEA

could. (Ha ha.)   Little meatballs cooked at high temps.
If your nipple ever got stuck to an icy pole, you could get it.

(3)

Seriously, don't hug your laptop!   Cocktails.   Sugar.
Smokes.   Anything that might comfort you might.

Except cannabis, aid to the cure if not the prevention. (Paid For
By The State Of Colorado.)   Then there's seaweed

harvested from radioactive oceans.   Swimming in radioactive
waves (or particles).   Eating fish with hidden lesions

and missing eyes.   Your bra could, your abortion, your
implants.   Your genes could be responsible.   Ask yourself:

How long do I want to live?   How can I do things
differently?   What am I doing wrong?

What, Me?

During the blizzard I ached with precognition: our souls, linked
   trapeze artists, our watches dangling in the icy continuum,
   our anti-gravitational loose change rising.

There's destiny in our future. I can't help but worry we're
   somehow sinking, even sunk—in the midst of all this
   (frippery), we're headed for a kind of disguised cliff.

When I worry, I worry I am wasting supposed time, or that if
   there is a being of some unimaginably sentient proportion
   with a lovely plan, I am a little idiot.

When one of us shines, I have the urge to yank the shiny one to
   the side of the stage. I worry someone will see the light and
   shoot at it.

I worry about words: *breast* and *landlocked* and *lucky,* words
   I've distilled right out of this poem in an effort to preserve
   essence.

I worry that you will not move to my state and I will not move
   back to your state and that our states will suffer irreparable
   worry on our behalf.

Worry is a darkroom where negatives are developed, they say,
   and I am a photograph awash in black water.

Pavane for a Dead Princess (at IKEA)

Once upon a wintry time in Colorado, we drove our 4WD to IKEA

in a softly accumulating Scandinavian snow to buy IKEA

paraphernalia to assemble back home, if we ever *got* back home. *IKEA!*

we said lovingly, for Sweden, perhaps, for the sexy architectural
   designs IKEA

touts in its tautological showrooms that led us around until the word
   IKEA

rang like Satan's surname and we knew ourselves defeated, senses
   stuffed IKEAlly

with faux real wood and a New Year's brunch made only in IKEA's

kitchen (*kök*) by snowshoeshod chefs famous for their IKEAn

spices (*kryddor*). We circled without hope or escape hatch, IKEA-

betrothed, valiant rats mazed-out on tiny meatballs, O, IKEA,

when, suddenly and without warning, we broke free from that fractal
   (IKEA)

into a day that had changed to a night, look!, frothy with fog, and
   without IKEA's

dazzling disastrous dross. Stunned by freedom, frantic from IKEA, we carried our booty away from that measuring(dip)stick, IKEA,

into parking structures, onto icy highways, promising never to darken
    IKEA's

lustrosity again. But we did, the way humans wander into oblivion
    (see IKEA)

of textile and futon in the kingdom of IKEA, then peer back, unabashed.

Psalm 1.0

Dear lord I have a good idea. I'm

at the end of the best thing ever.

The fact that I can see you at the

same time as the most beautiful

girl in the world is not the same

thing as too much of anything. I

have a great way of saying that I

don't know how much I love the

newspaper. I'm so excited about

this. I love the new version. I have

no idea what I'm saying. Dear

lord I have no idea why I'm still

waiting for you to be able to see

my tweets. I'm at the end of a

sudden urge to go home and sleep

all night. And you are a lot more fun

than a month ago. I don't think you

should be a little too hard and fast

food and water in the morning. I'm

not a fan of yours truly. I'm at a

news conference that I don't think

I have a lot to do with. The new

update is so good to me that I don't

know how to get my money back

in time. I love the way you are the

same as I am, but it doesn't matter

how hard I try. It's a little too late

for the rest of my life.

Tit, with Cannabis

That's my kind of chemo, someone says. (Not me, of course.)
(But if it were me, so what?) I'm colder than a witch's tit

in a brass bra on The Carousel of Happiness in Nederland,
Colorado, and you're here beside me, Ginsberg, giddy

with your rainbow of transcendental verses, your
festive little marijuana dispensary. Tonight the witch's tit

is a puckered blob. It's missing whole centimeters
of bright cold titness, wilting glacially in its old snow globe

or warming on the windowsill beside the irrational pi(e). Now
it shimmers in its unreconstructed self, abides transcendentally

in the gloaming, cancer and cannabis sprouting o'er the land.

Planes Fly in Formation over the Backyard, as in War Movies

Forever is so unfathomable it cannot be held responsible.

Or it is the joyful repetition of the increased effect of sun at high
    altitudes.

Meanwhile, birds are wise in thin air but live such a short time.

One lies broken in the snow; others surround it, screeching.

Normally I would say there are no images for infinity, but today I am
    not so sure.

Infinity flows in a blood-red path to itself.

(War spills infinitely into other wars.)

Five planes fly in formation over my backyard, as in war movies.

In reality, I kneel beside this infinite bird.

I am nothing but a string of bells, the hand of a minor god.

I will walk in snow four more times before spring arrives in the foothills.

Snow of burial and keening jays—the opposite of forever.

Latitudes

Summer Solstice

With that pink-ass moon in Sagittarius beaming obscenely
on the Flatirons, ruffling up infamy, you'd think citizens

would be howling to get out of their homes or booking
Groupons to wherever or philosophizing along a continuum

that might present itself for a stroll into euphoria. Or luck.
I don't know. We're supposed to stay the course, stay

embodied, check out our personal and collective delusions.
I walked my Chihuahua at dawn and a shirtless archer

appeared around a corner with a Great Dane at his side.
We all froze and looked at one another in a kind of rose-

tinted astonishment. Then the Chihuahua growled low,
the archer laughed, and the whole moon vanished in the sun.

Boulder Sonnets, with Buddha and Ginsberg

Some say sex is a product of light traveling at its own speed across the Rockies. Some that it occurs when the creek winds down to the pace of a Buddhist, bicycling. My left breast is a fine specimen of genetic codes and misappropriation. I wobble asymmetric, right breast holed up like a nun in a monastery. It's true, I haven't had sex once since arriving in Boulder, I tell my friend Ginsberg, who's lighter than hydrogen, sparkly as a jukebox. The Buddha in my backyard places poppies on my disembodied breast. Sex, he says, is light blazing boldly before it blows itself out.

Or sex is death traveling so fast it almost catches up with light. *Ha*, says Ginsberg, *Ha Ha Ha Ha*. It's true, I haven't had sex in Boulder, but I have had summer. My right breast is the queen of breasts, my left an old lover. Ginsberg and I foxtrot around a field of sunflowers. We waltz through our own ghosts. Bright crayons scribble all over our minds. Cancer sleeps beside us, a lustrous marble, a trippy chute. The Buddha in my backyard ignores both breasts equally, the living and the gone. Sex is a product of light observing itself twinkle, he says. Twinkling.

Summer Theater

A woman who sleeps with a nightlight is more likely to get breast cancer than a woman who sleeps in the dark. (AMA)

Act 1

Cancer, played by Anonymous, stage whispers to a rapt audience:

Quick, before she rewinds her circadian clock.

Ha ha, I proclaim, pleased to be played by anyone but myself.

I can't tell if I'm really laughing, but I assume I am, much like I assume there will be snow on Longs Peak at summer's end. (An aside.)

Nox, umbra, obscurum vitae. (Someone says.)

Cancer exists is either a false statement or no statement at all, according to philosophers who portray themselves, stage right, pondering the existence of the (orchestra) pit, currently seething with sound.

Buddha, played by the Jack Kerouac School of Disembodied Poetics, sits idly by, cracking codes of dark and light.

The orchestra strikes a nocturnal snore.

My bones sleep, propped up in the nightlight dark.

Act 2

Of night and light and the half-light

    —W. B. Yeats

Buddha, as himself,
enters silently in bike

shorts and helmet,
sits down beside me,

stage left, where I'm
having a near-death

experience before
a live audience.

Buddha nods (off).

Colorado Ties for 6th Sunniest State

(1)

I will not be buried in Elizabethport nor
one of the Oranges like the rest of my clan.

My body will not be flown home in a crate
to be clucked over by who knows which

Irish relatives. The way the sun rises here,
clanging its huge cowbell, easing the East

right out of you, you'd think everybody'd
be tinted silt and rouge and worshipping

The Bright Solar Prince of the Solar Palace.

(Who?) I'm but one who recently drifted
from old Jersey, the 27th sunniest state

where the sun shines 56% of the time. Don't
underestimate the operatic trill and maw

of this western sun as it blazes over you and
laughs behind the Rockies. It will draw you

to it and sear you like a steak, Jersey woman,
Golden Guernsey, little pail of milk.

(2)

Eggcream, potsy, stickball, stoop.

These are some of the words I've forgotten
under the influence of the Colorado sun.

(3)

My musical body will be buried beside the
Rockies beneath the lid of a baby grand
piano, my soul accompanied into the after-
life by a flashmob of multigenerational
percussionists.

(4)

All present will remember me as alive.

Nederland

Today I mixed burnt sienna with alizarin crimson and a sagey
green I call *everlasting*. I played with that trio a long time,

as long as I needed to get lost in the mind of color. I'm
such a messy painter, preferring fingers to brush, water play

to impasto. Now I find myself starting to riff, the way I often
grab ink and scribble words all over a painting. This one

is black and turquoise—with brown madder, the color of
blood. Which reminds me of a trip I took up a mountain

after surgery. Those colors followed me all the way up,
vibrating around my head like indefatigable lovers.

I thought: Someday I will make love to each and every one.

Boulder Sonnet, with Buddha and Crickets

I've never seen the words *fucking crickets* in a poem before, have you? *Creak creak scritch creak.* Buddha soaks up sun beside me while the crickets scratch religiously. (How does he do it?) A bee strolls along his lotused leg and the crickets go silent for one brief second between chirps: a mad caesura. Now rabbits run by, grinning with rabbit fever, the little snipers. Bunnies at Halloween? Isn't that like gourds at Easter? Our boisterous bugs seem summoned by a silence that longs to be filled—like the silence before these words. Aspens turn deftly to yellow light. Buddha's back's so still, you could write a poem on it.

Psalm 2.0

Dear lord I don't know what I was

just thinking about you but I'm still

in bed with my life and death and

destruction and a few years ago

I was just in my head and shoulders.

I love it when people say they will

not let you down. I have no clue

who you are. The fact is that I

have no clue who I am. I just have

a little more time with the stars

and I don't think you should be

able to do that to me. I'm so tired

of being the only one who can

make a difference in the morning.

I have a lot more to do with my

life and death and destruction and

a few days to get my nails done.

I can see you at the end of this

month. The only way to the gym

today is with my new phone and

it will not let me go.

My Daughters among Dragonflies

In the midst of a hundred maybe a thousand dragonflies,
I bring my daughters before the god of children

and demand an audience. I have a right to demand, after all.
I'm not the only one who brought them here, am I?

                                    To the giver of breath
I say: Lead them swiftly through a thousand dragonflies.

To the architect of womb and nipple: Keep them safe.

                            Once, on an el platform in Chicago,
I stood in the midst of dragonflies heading west.

Now I'm West and the dragonflies are giddy with sun,
circling silently around me as if I were a blooming lilac tree.

Were they always headed toward this future me, my arms
outstretched, heart bombarding heaven?

I think in spirals;

therefore,

I am infinite.

Back/words: 1999

My mother once said that the last thing she's worried about is whether or not she'll be a good bowler in her next life.

I hadn't seen her in three and half weeks. I'd gone away to Michigan to write poems about her then I'd gotten the flu and meanwhile she began to die in earnest. After all those months of being with her—eighteen—I missed the last three weeks of her life. I thought it would take so much longer. I arrived Wednesday night. At 3 a.m. she vomited and we changed her pajamas. I put a top on her the way they do in the hospital, backwards, and noticed she was burning up—felt like 105 fever. I changed her Depends. Then my Dad was knocking on my bedroom door again. This time it was diarrhea but it wasn't really, it was her death beginning, her system shutting down and we didn't know it. She was still burning beneath the backwards-on pajama top, but when I slipped the thermometer under her arm it only read 101. We gave her water with blue sponges on sticks, cold water, and wiped away something dark red that blotched her lips from dehydration. Little flakes of it got on her teeth and I picked them off and she sucked so hard on the sponges, then would hold them between her teeth and not let go. We finally called Sandy the second hospice nurse in command who got her totally clean and quote comfortable unquote and examined her and said her bowels were empty but still I didn't think anything unusual but Sandy had also taken her vitals so she called us—Dad & me—into the kitchen and said Mom might die soon. Today she said or maybe a week. (?) I asked her if I should call Zoe and Frank Jr. to tell them to come down here from Chicago or Melissa from next door but Sandy said not yet. So I thought we had time and Mom seemed comfortable and I made Dad some bacon and he made a waffle and I had an egg and a bagel and then I thought I should take a shower and wash my hair in case Mom died that night. Gerri the head hospice nurse arrived at 2:15

p.m. and took Mom's pulse and blood pressure. They were almost non-existent. My mother had been dying in the bedroom all by herself while I took my shower. Then Dad and Gerri and I got around Mom. We put on piano music—because I wanted Mom to relax—what an idiot I was—Mom's eyes were open the whole time but not focused and she was breathing very hard. Gerri said Mom would be going soon and we talked about the birds (our wild birds) and Dad was saying something about the grackles she loved and I stopped him and told him to get in close and hold Mom because I'd noticed she'd taken a long time between two inhalations. He turned to her and she took one more breath. Then a few minutes more, another. We were both crying. I didn't feel her go or anything like that but there had been a visual change a few minutes before her last breath. I thought maybe her spirit had left then and her body still breathed on for a few moments. We sat with Mom for a while and the priest arrived and said some prayers because it was too late for the Sacrament of the Sick, although she'd already had that several times. The prayers were comforting. When Dad started to cry again Father John got choked up too. Gerri was at Mom's feet. I was at her side on the bed beside her enormous rib cage. Then I guess Dad went out with the priest, and Gerri and I began to get Mom ready. Gerri washed her face. I held Mom's bones close to me when Gerri washed her bottom. We put on a white cotton nightgown and combed her hair but we couldn't get her mouth closed and we had trouble with the eyelids too, they'd close but then drift open again after a few seconds. Then Melissa came in—she was upset that she'd missed Mom's death. I think we'd had so many false alarms—from day one—that we just didn't believe she'd be dying today. I went out to sit in the van with Stephanie and the new baby, Cassie. I'd never met Cassie, she was nine days old, and then, really fast, the funeral guys came, Kevin and Randy, and talked details with my Dad and I hated them. Jonathan (who's two) had arrived with Dan and Megan and when I said to Randy, isn't

Jonathan great (which he is) Randy said—I've got one at home just like him—and I said under my breath, not like him, you don't. Then Kevin and Randy wrapped my Mom up like a corpse and took her out of the house on a stretcher with a royal blue robe over her face, put her in a van and drove away.

for Joan Marice Seaton, born September 24, 1926,
in Elizabeth, NJ; died April 29, 1999,
in Pinckneyville, IL, of metastatic breast cancer.

—Written the night of April 29, 1999

Sweet World

Wonder what I'd be today if I was still married to my Wall Street
husband besides married to a Wall Street husband and puking gin

in a silk sheath outside Delmonico's. I might be a size 4. I might
be a secret Democrat or a weekend lesbian. This morning five planes

flew over the yard in a V as I was about to dig into a pile of lavender
pancakes al fresco. The V flew low and slow. It flew loud and ominous.

It alarmed me, sounding a lot like the war movies of my fifties' childhood.
My cranky Chihuahua was proverbially biting at flies and I sat there

not thinking about hate. Recently, I experienced life with cancer. An
intoxicating time, richly infused with the liquor of death, but good too

because no one expected much of me and I was left to my own mind,
which is what I'm missing most these days. Unless that's it over there,

screeching on two wheels around the racetrack. Today I typed *gnos*
instead of *song* and I wondered if it was some new app designed

to mess with me. I've never thought to call the world sweet before.
Surviving something can do that, make things taste different.

Suddenly you're a hero/ine. All this devastation—
and you're still standing in the middle of it.

20 Little Lyric Essays (for *Harold and Maude*)

It's worth watching *Harold and Maude* again for that moment when Harold looks at the camera and you know he knows you know.

It's worth watching *Harold and Maude* again to say *Vivian Pickles*.

It's worth watching *Harold and Maude* again for Maude's favorite funeral umbrella, which is yellow.

It's worth watching *Harold and Maude* again for cemeteries, their breathtaking algorithmic symmetry and their stalkers.

It's worth watching *Harold and Maude* again for: *A lot of people enjoy being dead. But they are not dead, really.* Wisdom à la Maude.

Or this: *Grab the shovel, Harold.*

It's worth watching *Harold and Maude* again knowing that Ruth Gordon didn't die until she was 88, and on her last morning she was working on a play.

It's worth watching *Harold and Maude* again knowing Bud Cort is still alive and dimpling in the summer of 2016.

It's worth watching *Harold and Maude* again for the Cat Stevens controversies that have nothing and just about everything to do with music.

Maude tells Harold there are two things no human being should live without: making music and breaking the law. It's worth watching *Harold and Maude* again to see how they accomplish both.

It's worth watching *Harold and Maude* again to understand the difference between death and death, and to decide which one you prefer.

Death is a metaphor, of course, but for what? It's worth watching *Harold and Maude* again to find out.

It's worth watching *Harold and Maude* again to support or reverse the theory you've harbored your entire life about old women and sex.

Harold grows in wisdom over the course of *Harold and Maude*, but it's worth watching it again to see Harold's face when Maude says she took the pills two hours before her 80th birthday party.

What!? (Harold)

It's worth watching *Harold and Maude* again if you are on the fence about choosing your own death or about how old is old enough or whether you should move to Oregon or Vermont before it's too late.

It's worth watching *Harold and Maude* again to see Harold dance on a cliff. Or Bud Cort dance on a cliff. Either way, any movie with someone dancing on a cliff is worth watching again.

Maude was my great-grandmother's name, but without the *e*. Maud Emerson. Not necessarily a reason to watch *Harold and Maude* again, unless you like the way your mind travels from one Maude to the other, which I do.

And it's worth watching *Harold and Maude* again to recall that smart people exist. This is particularly comforting when any humanity your country still has left is up for grabs, not to mention its poetry.

For poetry alone, it is worth watching *Harold and Maude* again.

The History of the World Is a Palindrome

In the history of the world I appear as a dot in a turquoise
Chevrolet, one breast missing, the other smarter than six

months before when it lost its twin. Of the Chevy, historians
offer scant reflection. Of the erstwhile breast, none. The light

that flickers faithfully inside the turquoise dot, as if caught
communicating memory in code—from Morse to semaphore

to dance—is an unsolvable mystery in the history of the
world, as all light has tended to be since the beginning of time,

whenever that was, or, more accurately, whenever that will be.

Immortal #9

1

Immortality does not normally appeal to me, although magic squares seem innocent enough.

$$4 \quad 9 \quad 2$$
$$3 \quad 5 \quad 7$$
$$8 \quad 1 \quad 6$$

2

Of my nine muses—Sally Field, Olive Oyl, the Sargasso Sea, the IRT, Stevie Wonder, Fibonacci, robots, Pthalo blue, and Yoko—all but one have appeared to me in a poem uninvited.

3

The number nine is not a prime number, but I don't hold that against it.

4

There are nine underground worlds (Aztec), nine circles of hell (Dante), and nine months of summer (Miami).

5

Nine o's in the combined names of Yoko Ono Lennon and John Ono Lennon.

6

Ah! Böwakawa poussé, poussé. (9 syllables)

7

The Ennead (nine Egyptian deities) decided who could be born and who could pass on to the afterlife. See also: nine Supreme Court judges.

8

The Peacemaker Enneagram, Type 9, is the type of many famous people—e.g., Carl Jung, Whoopi Goldberg, Ringo.

9

Finally, the Norse god, Odin, hung himself on an ash tree for nine days to learn the runic alphabet and teach it to humanity. Who would care that much about language, I ask myself while singing so loud you can hear me all the way to the ninth (defunct) planet. It's there that the peacemakers find me, there where they call my name.

Pavane for a Dead Princess (on Pluto)

July 14, 2015. The New Horizons space probe, en route for over nine years, finally passed Pluto, where a handful of Clyde W. Tombaugh's ashes was tossed from the flyby in commemoration of his 1930 discovery.

She wonders if Clyde Tombaugh (her hero) is as pissed off
as she is over his demoted discovery. Maybe he's content

with cold truth, she thinks, however it evolves. She marks
the day his ashes will catapult through the dwarf's icy belt,

makes plans to be alone on top of one of the Twin Sisters,
bundled with stars dying in her hair, as Pluto and its moons

shimmer into view for the flyby, then roll away like snowballs.
Perhaps there's another world she might reach, she thinks,

by rowboat. Or undercover. Mercy on the other side.

The Astonished

Like lovers, the astonished remain silent for years at a time.

Their meals are cunnilingual: starfruit, fennel, cream of coconut palm.

Their voices resemble the sugar-scented acoustics of children.

Praise flows toward them and away, for the astonished are spun of hope.

They meld universes—ours and theirs and theirs and others.

They look forward to the day when blood will rise into clogged water,

                    when everything ever known has blown away.

Sometimes a woman maroons herself on the Island of Astonishment.

(If she remembers how.) (If her body can navigate time.)

The astonished watch her land in trees the size of worlds.

They love her until she dies or lives, whichever astonishes her more.

Tit, with Foreplay

I too would like the leisurely mind of men.

I would hold my mind in my own two hands and pet it.

If I could be anything it would be a composer.

The one who provides the soul.

Not the body, all modulated and linguistic.

Play, they call it. Play.

Or, not the mind of men. The leisurely mind of God.

Which reminds me of the mind of music.

Which reminds me of the mind of sex.

I would write an oratorio.

Me. Your lovely mate with the fickle surviving breast.

I predict a pause in this musical composition, a shift in the direction
of time.

All along, I've meant to hold music in my hand and give it to you.

Tit, with Blue Guitar

Once upon a blue guitar, the right tit rested while

the left oversaw the heart. Sure, she loved their duet,

their symmetry and silk, Stevie Nicks, Christine McVie,

getting older but still getting it on.

                                    Now some say

she's harmoniously flawed. As if a left tit in the trough

means she's a has-been musician who can't strap a guitar

across her ribs or peak at squeaky sweet soprano highs

like she used to, rising up and up to the zone where

nothing matters but God and the moment, all music

and imagining, sex and oscillation, right tit soloing a riff

a cappella.

The Integrity of Matter; or, Peace in the Rose-colored Now

There's blood on the page before this one. See?
The dark kicks up. Air torques. Rain tasers the skin.

What did Ginsberg say? That he wrote poems to tell
his version of things in a world that only tells versions

of power? How many days do we have, really?
A tornado touches down in the next town north.

My heart iambs to some ancient classic—maybe Jackson
Brown, maybe Stylistics. I totter at St. Vrain Creek

where it bursts from the Rockies. Cottonwoods catch me.
When the child who lives in this house is away his toys

grieve. Thomas the Train is speechless and the mottled
ball sits still. I forget the name of the film where a woman

walks into walls in hopes of entering the womb of an atom.
The child's atoms are here, even as he climbs into the next

plane home. What a big open space I am. The way these
electrons come together, you'd think I was real.

The Integrity of Matter (A Footnote)

Whether it be your own body's matter
or an unanimated body's matter
(as in stone), the integrity of all matter
is related to the fact that matter,

animated or unanimated, does matter,
which jibes with the fact that all matter,
stone, flesh, or combo, will matter
infinitely—that is, without end (a matter

of speculation), although facts of matter
existing in bodies, even stones, matter
less than the actual end of matter,
which, to a stone's integrity, will matter

less than to yours—for you, animated matter,
care greatly about whether (or not) you matter.

A Distillation of Matter

Distilled linearly from Susan Griffin's
Woman and Nature, "Book One: Matter"

God
is

a sensual fact
no more no less

nor nightmares
nor chamber music

mathematical law
universally valid

the brain on the summit
of the backbone

a product of warfare
the chatter of apes

12,170

tendencies to occur
like foreign bodies

her red hair loose
down her back

The Color of Oxygen

I'm that woman in the Agatha Christie novel relaxing in an oxygen bar
off Pearl Street. I suspect myself of murder, yet I'm presumed innocent

by all who see me: Buddhists, skateboard kids, musicians sharing
marijuana mints on the corner. Or, I'm that woman, but I'm on a train

between Denver and Chicago, and my smart tortoise shell compact contains
a powder that, when inhaled, kills instantly. If I try to recall what I envision

while connected to O_2, I might tell you a stranger in a scarlet tie (a
clue)—not blue, as you might expect from someone high on air. I've often

been considered incapable of wrongdoing by most, so non-threatening,
not someone engaged in espionage, sex, the sweet settling of scores.

Now all these homicidal musings have made me nervous, as if I foresee
my own future while breathing benign gas in a city that prides itself on its

bubble of wellbeing. Which leads me to the color red (the true color
of oxygen). As soon as I catch my breath, I'll summit a nearby peak

with its craggy face that looks out serenely over the rest of the world
and doesn't give a flying fuck if anyone makes it to the top or not.

Avoiding Suicide: A Grandmother Poem

A loomy mountain looms outside the window, waves to me from a great height. A small boy jumps off the mountain and lives! (I'm hallucinating.) In reality, I bounce around in a bouncy house with the little daredevil, champion toddler jumper of Boulder County, who flips and falls as if made of cloud. (Logic has no place here, nor the gross motor skills of a woman high on altitude.) Thus the poem augurs an undecipherable path. It leaps along the mountaintop. Stop using me in your ridiculous death scenarios, interjects the mountain, which is rocky, after all, not all that secure in its footing or self-esteem. (More hallucinating.) Other Rockies leap around me like a dozen redeeming boys.

Notes on Ash Wednesday

Against the Word the unstilled world still whirled
About the centre of the silent Word.

    —T. S. Eliot

Skin shedding like notes down a harp.
How we once had sex on the head of a drum.
Light to the elements, light to the infinite gift of breasts.
Oh, we never had sex on a drum, but we could have. We made sound.

Soon to the portal of old age, the two of us groaning as we lift the grandkid.
(Your Brooklyn *fucks* don't sound so hip on the lips of a two-year-old.)
Jesus Christmas. (Neither of us has ever said this before, ever.)
Still, look at the way your body moves at sixty.

My polestar, you bend in halftime to kiss me.
Mozey, you say, standing on your head, your silky dreads
swaying upside down. There will be a day when our skin is parchment, our

eyes the only part we recognize. Holy cows and horses along the way
will salute us as we pass them for the last time. Delicious
dying day. Our bodies smoky and soft as ash.

First They Were

... a fleet of owls, throwing the hoot between them,
owls with two faces singing Ave and Ouch Ave and Ouch ...

    —Alice Oswald

Then they were a stampede of bees—thorax, mandible, antennae—
gleaming steadfast and wailing like trains from old centuries.

Or they were a smatter of souls begging for change along
the off-ramp. Or a trace of fragile half-lives, or the almost

ghosts of whole lives yearning for continuance. And me?
First I was an ordinary woman—clavicle, femur, pelvis—

every bone predictable inside my spandex skin. Then
I was a thought experiment, living and dead, there and here,

stranded between horizons, like a centaur or a saint. If you'd
known me then, you might have wondered at my sugar maple

hair, my Klee tattoo, how I walked through seas hitching my skirt,
singing *Ave and Ouch Ave and Ouch*, the dust of my old self
    dispersing.

12 Paintings from Hollis Sigler's *Breast Cancer Journal*

Miami, 2016

The woman holds a fan above her head. She has

painted two paintings—the cause and the cure.

Everything's in twos except her and the fan. The

easels, the paintings, the sconces and their yel-

low lights, streams of water cascading. She has

two arms, two legs, and it looks (although it's not

clear) that she still has two breasts.

Here the birds have turned into knives around a

blue dress. There's a hat on a rack, long billowy

curtains, a desk with an old-fashioned telephone,

and a table with more knives. Someone we can't

see has left the room. The door is open a few

inches. Or else the dress itself has come in, and

upon entering was attacked by birds as knives.

There is a royal blue pillow on a hot pink chair.

Mountains look like pointy breasts. Two chairs

and an old TV cabinet. She was a year younger

than I was but she's been dead for as long as I've

taught poetry in Florida. It's good to wait as long

as you can to get cancer. Then it's good to take a

long time before you get it again and then again.

While you wait you can live your life.

In this painting the trees have been mended and
birds soar in colors around a peaceful scene with
a purple sky, and I remember the first time I saw
a Hollis Sigler painting back in Chicago—how
color was everywhere, even on the frame. This is
a painting to rest in. It says: Rest for a while. We
are all going to die.

I don't want to look at this one but I will tell you that the room itself (the iconic room of Sigler fame) has been partly painted away and there are five vignettes of possible cancer causes painted over the room, where there is only one chair and no dresses and no women. It is not a pretty pic-ture. That's the point.

In this one there are dresses all over a hill that lead to a woman at the top. Six red birds holding the banner with Sigler's sentence in longhand. The woman is chastely naked and has two breasts, although from this distance it is impossible to tell if they are real or reconstructed. When asked if I would like reconstruction, I promptly said no. I'd been thinking about my answer for a long time—maybe 15 years. Maybe more. I also thought I would have someone tattoo my scar if I ever had one, but, as it turns out, I don't believe that's going to happen. The tattoo, that is.

Birds again, this time in the frame. Hats on display, and blouses. Two stars. I went to the doctor yesterday, but there are no blood tests for metastatic breast cancer. You just have to wait. After the doctor's I went to look at a house for rent in Miami. The woman who lived there had hung a half dozen dresses to dry in a small tree in her backyard.

She really has nothing left to lose. (H.S.)

There's a question mark at the top of a rainbow.

Arms with wings holding back curtains. Broken

things, a webbed chair. The waiting is not fun.

The way cancer lives in there, walking around

your body like it belongs, is odder than many

things, and there are many odd things: God.

Emus. Handcuffs. Celery. History. Blood.

Nightgown, dresses, pants, jackets. Trees and
vanities. A hill again, a statue at the top. The par-
ty is over in this painting. The parade is over. The
fashion show is over. The heroine has departed.
The cancer, writes Sigler, *is now in my bones, my*
pelvis, and my spine. I wonder where mine is
headed. Someday I will tell you.

In this painting women appear to be walking up

a lighted driveway. About halfway up they sprout

wings.

Meanwhile, a hurricane has passed Miami by. It feels strange, like we've all been jilted. This painting has its own cyclone rising from a small table containing food and utensils. There was once a woman in this room.

The Last Prairie

They say this is a hawthorn tree, but why should I believe them? Who named it and who names *cold* when the sun shifts behind the moon's closed face? I loved a woman who refused to believe in museums. She stood before a Diebenkorn and said: "How do I know this is a Diebenkorn?" Similarly, I sight a red-tailed hawk higher than the Navy jet that flies above the prairie and ask: How do I know this is a red-tailed hawk? I've seen the aurora borealis as far south as Connecticut. I've seen slugs mating and my own blood on the tip of a six-inch needle. I've seen three people born, two, my daughters, one the son of a friend. My friend's blood on my white leather Keds. I've danced wildly in a cathedral. Stood at the mouth of a cave and seen the frozen breath of God. I've seen a tornado leap over my house. A pileated woodpecker, a handful of chickadees. I was awakened once by a mockingbird snoring outside my bedroom window. Now I'm here on the last prairie searching for an endangered bird of prey with the odd shortcoming of no talons. He looks like Zorro. They say he impales his victims on the long thorns of the hawthorn tree. Here is the grove of hawthorn trees. Here is the field mouse pretending not to notice. Twenty feet below are roots that feed us. When we die we'll ache with thirst, then survive.

Notes

"Avoiding Suicide: A Grandmother Poem," "Boulder Sonnet, with Buddha and Crickets," "Boulder Sonnets, with Buddha and Ginsberg," "The Color of Oxygen," "Colorado Ties for 6th Sunniest State," "Notes on Ash Wednesday," "Planes Fly in Formation over the Backyard, as in War Movies," "Summer Theater," "Tit, with Cannabis," and "Tit, with Foreplay" all owe a debt to the late Jim Simmerman. Each began as raw material from his magical prompt, "Twenty Little Poetry Projects."

"Tit, with Shelf Life" ends with a quote from Ram Dass's *Be Here Now.*

"Pavane for a Dead Princess (at IKEA)" and "Pavane for a Dead Princess (on Pluto)" take their titles from Maurice Ravel's *Pavane pour une infante défunte,* composed in 1899, of which he wrote: *Do not be surprised, that title has nothing to do with the composition. I simply liked the sound of those words and I put them there, c'est tout.*

"Psalm 1.0" and "Psalm 2.0" were composed entirely with iPhone's Suggestion Bar.

"20 Little Lyric Essays (for *Harold and Maude*)" is for Colin Higgins (1941–1988) and after Jim Simmerman (1952–2006). As of 2016, physician-assisted suicide is legal in Colorado as well as in Vermont and Washington State.

"The Astonished" is for Holly Iglesias.

"Notes on Ash Wednesday" is for Lori Anderson.

Acknowledgments

The Adroit Journal: " I Dreamt a Land of Someone Else's Invention"
(as "Whiteout")

Bellevue Literary Review: "Tit, with Shelf Life," "Two Men Walking a
Breast"

Bloom: "Boulder Sonnets, with Buddha and Ginsberg"

Court Green: "Avoiding Suicide: A Grandmother Poem"

Diode: "Pavane for a Dead Princess (on Pluto)"

Fence: "The Last Prairie"

MIPOesias: "Tit, with Cannabis"

Nashville Review: "Boulder Sonnet, with Buddha and Crickets"

Painted Bride Quarterly: "Colorado Ties for 6th Sunniest State" (as
"West Ho" and "West Ho 2")

Pleiades: "Psalm 1.0" (as *"from* The Book of Six (Suggestions)")

Plume: "The Color of Oxygen," "What, Me?"

PoetsArtists: "The History of the World Is a Palindrome"

Posit Journal: "Tit, with Foreplay," "The Integrity of Matter," "The
Integrity of Matter (A Footnote)," "Psalm 2.0," "Immortal #9"

Rhino: "Tit, with Blue Guitar"

Sinister Wisdom: "12 Paintings from Hollis Sigler's *Breast Cancer
Journal*" (as "The Drama of the Departed Heroine"), "A
Distillation of Matter," "Notes on Ash Wednesday"

Superstition Review: "Planes Fly in Formation over My Backyard, as in
War Movies," "Sweet World"

Tammy: "The Carousel of Happiness: A Stereogram"

Waxwing: "20 Little Lyric Essays (for *Harold and Maude*)," "Latitudes"

"Tit, with Shelf Life" and "Two Men Walking a Breast" were reprinted in *Bared*, Femmes Folles Books, 2016, Laura Madeline Wiseman, ed.

"Boulder Sonnet, with Buddha and Crickets," "Boulder Sonnets, with Buddha and Ginsberg," "Colorado Ties for 6th Sunniest State" (as "West Ho"), "The Last Prairie," "Psalm 1.0" (as *from* The Book of Six"), "Tit, with Cannabis," "Tit, with Shelf Life," "Two Men Walking a Breast," and "What, Me?" (as "What?!") appeared in the chapbook *Tit, with Blue Guitar*, from Dancing Girl Press, 2016.

These poems are also dedicated, with love and gratitude, to Emily, Jennifer, Matthew, Linda, Peni, Denise, Connie, Marsha, Steve, Mia, Holly, Sam, Sonny, Neil, Kristine, Carolina, Lori, and my beloved students and colleagues at the University of Miami; and to Joan Cusack Handler, for her beautiful life, love, poetry, and friendship; and, in memory, to two poets whose words have helped me navigate the dragonflies:

Audre Lorde (1934–1992) & Julia Darling (1956–2005).

CavanKerry's Mission

CavanKerry Press is committed to expanding the reach of poetry to a general readership by publishing poets whose works explore the emotional and psychological landscapes of everyday life.

Other Books in the LaurelBooks Series

This book was printed on paper from responsible sources.

Sweet World has been set in Fairfield, an old-style serif typeface designed in 1940 by Rudolph Ruzicka, a Czech-born American wood engraver.